The March to Love

Gaston Miron

The March to Love

Selected Poems

Edited by
Douglas G. Jones

Translations by Douglas G. Jones,
Marc Plourde, Louis Simpson, Brenda Fleet,
John Glassco and Dennis Egan

INTERNATIONAL POETRY SERIES
Volume X

Ohio University Press
Athens

Originally published as Volume X of the
Byblos Editions, International Poetry Forum,
in a limited edition of 300 copies.

The type is set in Elante, composed by Allegro Graphics.
Printed in the United States of America.

Grateful acknowledgment is made to the Department of External
Affairs of Canada for its assistance in the publication of this book, to
Les Presses de l'Université de Montréal and to Editions de l'Université
d'Ottawa for permission to reprint the original French texts and to
Guernica Editions for permission to reprint the Marc Plourde
translations from Embers and Earth.

Library of Congress Cataloging-in-Publication Data

Miron, Gaston, 1928–
  The march to love.

  (International poetry series ; v. 10)
  English and French
  1. Miron, Gaston, 1928–   —Translations, English.
I. Jones, Douglas G.   II. Title.   III. Series.
PQ3919.2.M5A25   1987   841   87–12264
ISBN 0–8214–0877–1
ISBN 0–8214–0878–X (pbk.)

The first book in the International Poetry Forum's Byblos Series was Marco Antonio Montes de Oca's *The Heart of the Flute* translated by Laura Villaseñor with an introduction by Octavio Paz. The second was Artur Lundkvist's *Agadir* translated and with an introduction by William Jay Smith and Leif Sjoberg. Yannis Ritsos' *Subterranean Horses* in a translation by Minas Savvas and with an introduction by Vassilis Vassilikos was the third selection. The fourth and fifth were Bulgarian selections published simultaneously: Lyubomir Levchev's *The Mysterious Man* translated by Vladimir Phillipov, and Cornelia Bozhilova's translation of Bozhidar Bozhilov's *American Pages*. *A Bird of Paper* was the sixth selection. This book had the additional distinction of being the result of close collaboration between the Nobel Laureate Vicente Aleixandre and his friends and translators Willis Barnstone and David Garrison. The seventh volume was *Transformations of the Lover* by Adonis (Ali Ahmed Said) translated by myself. Frederick H. Fornoff's translation of Laureano Albán's *The Endless Voyage* was the eighth Byblos selection. Gevorg Emin's *For You on New Year's Day*, translated by Diana Der Hovanessian, with an introduction by Yevgeny Yevtushenko and afterword by Edmond Y. Azadian, was the ninth Byblos Edition. This present volume is the tenth in the series and remains in the same tradition of providing translations of some of the most significant poets in the world for an audience that would not otherwise be able to read them.

> Samuel Hazo
> President/Director
> International Poetry Forum

INTRODUCTION

When Gaston Miron's collection of poems entitled *L'homme Rapaillé* appeared in Montreal in 1970, the critics unanimously agreed that the heart of Quebec had finally been given a voice.

We, the writers of Montreal, know the author through his frequent and vigorous discourses on poetry, Quebec and society. However, few of us have looked for him between the lines of his texts, being content to listen to him talk about any one of many burning issues or read his poems with their asymmetrical rhythm which lends itself so well to recitation.

What impressed his readers then and now was the original structure interwoven with new images and the particularly dramatic tone, in the Greek sense of the word, permeating every verse that he wrote.

Reading him takes one back many centuries to the beginnings of French poetry, to the time of Villon and Rutebeuf. Not only did Miron rediscover the direct, unadorned means of expression of the first French poets, but, at a deeper level, he found the connection with the great timeless mystery of poetry: the creation of live thought.

This little book that would soon bring its author a national and international reputation has earned the most prestigious awards in French and Canadian literature: the Guillaume Apollinaire Prize, which in 1981 put the crowning touch on the French Maspero edition, and in 1985, the Molson Prize from the Canada Council, recognizing the poet's important contribution to Quebec literature and its development.

Miron was born in Sainte-Agathe-des-Monts in 1928. He began writing at a very early age and published his first poems in the Montreal daily *Le Devoir*. In 1953, he published his first collection of poems jointly with another poet, Olivier Marchand. The following year he and a group of friends founded the Hexagone, a publishing house dedicated to poetry. From that time on he has been present wherever he could strike a blow for a national literature in Quebec.

The fact that his life is dedicated essentially to poetry is a powerful paradox that reveals the importance of poetry in the life of the man, and that of his life in his poetry. "The Pharisees," he wrote in 1965, "will never forgive me for being ashamed *with* everybody in spirit and in truth in my poetry, rather than being ashamed *of* everybody. Being ashamed with man at a gut level."

Poetry is the essential core of Miron's life, and a long process of ripening and integration with the world is required before a poem could take form, find its soul and be expressed. It is as if the poem and the vision of man that is expressed is embodied in the individual's struggle and survival. This accounts for the "anthropological survival" that is naturally a part of Miron's poetic adventure. More than politics, this vision is one of man as a whole (a nation cannot exist independently of the people that make it up). Miron seems to have renounced the brilliance and charm of an acquired literature and to have carefully cultivated his language and brought it back to life after centuries of colonization, alienation and stagnation. This is not an artificial life, but one that is animated by a collective spirit. And this produces a universal form of poetry which can be written only by one who has turned his back on an isolated literary adventure in preference for a literature of being. Heidegger used a simple formula to express existence: *in-der-welt-sein*; being-in-the world. Is it possible to exist in poetry, to make poetry a part of daily existence? This is the challenge that Miron accepts. In the course of years of political involvement, militancy and literary activity, the three being closely related, a few poems came forth, bringing imagery to light after years of dereliction and darkness in a revolutionary thrust that made it possible to advance towards love.

Miron is never concerned with the aesthetics of language. His poetry has a new form composed of words and images, sustained by experience rather than aesthetic emotion. This is a long, almost alchemical process that makes the poems so intense, so precious and so rare, transforming the vision into a substance that takes its life from the very life of the poet, as Jean Cocteau would have said. Such is the rarity of poetry that seeks not to please the author or the reader, but to make the world more real because it has more reality in it.

In the poetic process pursued by Miron, the personal drama is constantly identified with the collective, and the two are linked by the drama of the word. In the particularly tense context of this past twenty years in Quebec, the poet has succeeded in upholding together a vision of man, of being and of language to overcome the

[ii]

many forms of resistance and to see a being-in-the-world emerge independent and free.

The abyss between man and his world formed by years of self-colonialism had stifled any emergence of literature or any art form whatsoever.

By a transformation of life in its very principle, not by external verbal manipulation, the poetic art of Miron seeks to change the curve of things and events in order to make it luminous, joyful and supple under a government for whom freedom is essential to all human life. Before opacity can be transformed into light, into freedom and sanity, there has to be a language full of meaning. Where can such meaning be found, except in our origins? "Father and mother, you both had the knowledge to name everything there is on the earth . . ."

Three conditions must be met and combined with one another before this internal revolution can be completed, and none of them is sufficient by itself. First, there is the vision that must have its source and its strength in the conviction that every man possesses the universe in his spirit. Life must then find its natural rhythm and the full, unconstrained force of its expression and its dynamism. Finally, language will serve as the link between soul and existence, will inform life about the vision that it contains in potential and will give the vision the strength and power that it needs to affirm itself. When Miron says that he is "advancing his poetry," this is what he means; life and language progress and sustain each other to propose a solution to the drama of man, to end the universal and eternal conflict of man's exile in a land that he does not understand, in a kingdom that he does not rule.

The goal is to bring the conflict to its highest level, because the solution lies in the heart of the poems. It is from within that we will transform the world.

Guy Gervais
Literature Officer
Department of External Affairs of Canada

CONTENTS

Introduction   i

L'homme rapaillé   2 — Reintegrated   3

Extrait de *Courtepointes*   4 — From *Patchwork*   5

Les siècles de l'hiver   16 — The Reign of Winter   17

Fragment de la vallée   18 — Fragment of the Valley   19

Le verre d'eau
ou l'inacceptable   20 — A Glass of Water,
or the Unbearable   21

La braise et l'humus   22 — Embers and Earth   23

Ma désolée sereine   24 — My Sad One and Serene   25

Héritage de la tristesse   26 — Inheriting Distress   27

L'homme agonique   30 — The Agonized Man   31

Pour mon rapatriement   32 — For My Repatriation   33

Tête de caboche   34 — Hardheads   35

Il fait un temps fou   36 — The Weather Is Crazy   37

Poème de séparation   42 — Poem of Separation   43

Seul et seule   44 — Two Solitudes   45

Rue Saint-Christophe   46 — Rue Saint-Christophe   47

Art poétique   48 — The Art of Poetry   49

Le vieil Ossian   50 — Old Ossian   51

Après et plus tard   52 — Afterwards and Later   53

La marche à l'amour   54 — The March To Love   55

La corneille   74 — The Raven   75

Dans les lointains   76 — In the Far Out   77

L'octobre   78 — October   79

Compagnon des Amériques   80 — Companion of the Americas   81

Foyer naturel   84 — Natural Home   85

Le quatrième amour   86 — Fourth Love   87

L'ombre de l'ombre   88 — The Shadow's Shadow   89

La pauvreté anthropos   90 — La Pauvreté Anthropos   91

En une seule phrase nombreuse   92 — In One Grand Sentence   93

The March to Love

J'ai fait de plus loin que moi un voyage abracadabrant
il y a longtemps que je ne m'étais pas revu
me voici en moi comme un homme dans une maison
qui s'est faite en son absence
je te salue, silence

je ne suis pas revenu pour revenir
je suis arrivé à ce qui commence

REINTEGRATED

Abracadabra, I left myself behind and took a trip
a long time had gone by since I took stock of myself
I am back to myself like a man in a house
built in his absence
I salute you, silence

This time, not just for the sake of returning
I have arrived at a real beginning

For Emmanuelle   — *Tr. by Brenda Fleet*

Sentant la glaise
le sanglot
je m'avance ras
et gras, du pas
de l'escargot

à mon cou je porte
comme une amulette
un vertical néant

j'ai aussi, que j'ai
la vie comme black-out
sommeil blanc

*

Feeling the soil
the sobbing
I progress flat
and fat, pat in
a snail's pace

from the neck I cart
like an amulet
a vertical nothingness

I also have, that I have
life like a black-out
blanched slumber

*

C'est mon affaire
la terre et moi
flanc contre flanc

je prends sur moi
de ne pas mourir

*

It is my business
the earth and me
flank against flank

I take it upon myself
not to die

*

Nous sommes dans nos cloisons
comme personne n'a d'idée là-dessus

sur un mur le corps s'imprime
les yeux se font soupiraux

les yeux voient par en-dedans
à travers la tête éparse
monter le mercure de l'usure

mais je sais qu'elle y est
la lumière au recto des murs

elle travaille pour nous

un jour les murs auront mal
et ce qui adhère

nous verrons comment c'est   dehors

*

We are within our partitions
as no one can imagine

on a wall a body leaves its print
eyes form cellar windows

the eyes see from within
through a scattered head
the ascent of well-worn mercury

but I know that it is there
the light to the right of the walls

it works for us

one day the walls will ache
and that which sticks

we will see how it is   outside

*

C'est à voir
l'homme
le doigt dessus

aujourd'hui je m'avance
avec des preuves

*

It must be seen
mankind
the finger on it

today I progress
with evidence

*

Les mots nous regardent
ils nous demandent
de partir avec eux
jusqu'à perte de vue

*

The words are watching us
they are asking us
to leave with them
as far as the eye can see

*

Le monde ne vous attend plus
il a pris le large
le monde ne vous entend plus
l'avenir lui parle

*

The world no longer awaits you
it has gone out to sea
the world no longer listens to you
it appeals to the future

— *Tr. by Dennis Egan*

Le gris, l'agacé, le brun, le farouche
tu craques dans la beauté fantôme du froid
dans les marées de bouleux, les confréries
d'épinettes, de sapins et autres compères
parmi les rocs occultes et parmi l'hostilité

pays chauves d'ancêtres, pays
tu déferles sur des milles de patience à bout
en une campagne affolée de désolement
en des villes où ta maigreur calcine ton visage
nous nos amours vidées de leurs meubles
nous comme empesés d'humiliation et de mort

et tu ne peux rien dans l'abondance captive
et tu frissones à petit feu dans notre dos

Grey land and furious, brown and savage
split in the ghostly beauty of the cold
in tides of birch, in brotherhoods
of spruce and pine, and in your similars
of hidden rocks, of enmities

bare ancestral land, our land
over your infinite patient miles you are flowing
into a landscape maddened by loneliness
into the towns where famine chars your face
into our empty and unfurnished loves
and into us stiffened by restoration to your earth,
                                        our death

and you are helpless in this captive wealth of ours
you shiver
in this slow fire that is burning in our backs

— Tr. by John Glassco

Pays de jointures et de fractures
vallée de l'Archambault
étroite comme les hanches d'une femme maigre

diamantaire clarté
les échos comme des oiseaux cachés

sur tes pentes hirsutes
la courbure séculaire des hommes
contre la face empierrée des printemps montagneux

je me défais à leur encontre
de la longue lente prostration des pères

dans l'éclair racine nocturne
le firmament se cabre et de crête en crête
va la corneille au vol balourd

émouvante voix de balise

Country of jointures and fractures
Archambault Valley
narrow as the hips of a skinny woman

diamond-land clarity
echoes like concealed birds

on your coarse slopes
the secular curvature of men
against the stony face of mountainous springs

turning from them I free myself
from the long laggard prostration of fathers

in the lightening nocturnal root
the firmament rears and from crest to crest
veers the crow on clumsy wings

a beacon's moving voice

— Tr. by Dennis Egan

Les bourgeons de la soif dans les pores
ce n'est pas l'eau que je bois dans le verre
c'est quelque chose au fil de l'eau
à quoi on pense dans le roule des jours
comme un défoncé enfoncé
toute la sainte face de journée
toute, goutte à goutte
car la soif demeure, panique, tenace
car ni de poids, de place ou d'étendue
ni dedans, ou dehors peut-être
rien de rien n'est changé
j'ai toujours la motte de feu à l'estomac
je refuse à fond de mes deux pieds
sur les freins du temps
comme d'accoutumance chaque fois
une fois les yeux ouverts
et vide le verre

The thirst buds in my pores
are not for the glass of water I drink
but for something beyond water
something we think about as the hours tumble past
like a man who's been had through and through
all day the whole blessèd day
from drop to drop
because the thirst holds fast and panicky
and neither in weight, space or place
neither within nor without maybe
nothing in nothing has changed
I've always that fire in my stomach
and I say *no* down to the balls of my two feet
on the brakes of time
no, as always
once my eyes have opened
and the glass is empty

— *Tr. by Marc Plourde*

Rien n'est changé de mon destin ma mère mes camarades
le chagrin luit toujours d'une mouche à feu à l'autre
je suis taché de mon amour comme on est taché de sang
mon amour mon amour fait mes murs à perpétuité

un goût d'années d'humus aborde à mes lèvres
je suis malheureux plein ma carrure, je saccage
la rage que je suis, l'amertume que je suis
avec ce boeuf de douleurs qui souffle dans mes côtes

c'est moi maintenant mes yeux gris dans la braise
c'est mon coeur obus dans les champs de tourmente
c'est ma langue dans les étapes des nuits de ruche
c'est moi cet homme au galop d'âme et de poitrine

je vais mourir comme je n'ai pas voulu finir
mourir seul comme les eaux mortes au loin
dans les têtes flambées de ma tête, à la bouche
les mots corbeaux de poème qui croassent
je vais mourir vivant dans notre empois de mort

Nothing has changed in my life my mother my friends
sorrow still flickers from one firefly to the next
I am stained by my love as one is stained with blood
my love my love goes on forever building these walls

a taste of years of earth comes to my lips
backbreaking unhappiness is what I've got as I plunder
the rage that I am, the bitterness that I am
with this pain this ox breathing under my ribs

now these are my grey eyes in the embers
and my heart a mine in fields of torment
and my tongue in the cells in the hives of nighttime
this is me this man with his heart and soul at a gallop

I will die in a way I never wanted to die
alone and like the dead waters out there I will die
among the burnt heads in my skull, with the crow
words of a poem croaking in my mouth
I will die from living in this killing starch

— Tr. by Marc Plourde

Ma désolée sereine
ma barricadée lontaine
ma poésie les yeux brûlés
tous les matins tu te lèves à cinq heures et demie
dans ma ville et les autres
avec nous par la main d'exister
tu es la reconnue de notre lancinance
ma méconnue à la cime
tu nous coules d'un monde à l'autre
toi aussi tu es une amante avec des bras
non n'aie pas peur petite avec nous
nous te protégeons dans nos puretés fangeuses
avec nos corps revendiqués beaux
et t'aime Olivier
l'ami des jours qu'il nous faut espérer
et même après le temps de l'amer
quand tout ne sera que mémento à la lisière des ciels
tu renaîtras toi petite
parmi les cendres
le long des gares nouvelles
dans notre petit destin
ma poésie le coeur heurté
ma poésie de cailloux chahutés

My sad one and serene
my distantly withdrawn stream
my poetry with the snowblind eyes
every morning you get up at five
in my city and the others with you
drawn by the hand to survive
you are the image of our daily grind
my enigma of the far hillside
you sweep us from one world to the other
for you also have a lover's arms
don't be afraid little one with us
we will protect you with our murky purity
with our bodies beautifully redeemed
and Olivier loves you
friend of days for which we still must hope
even when the bitter time is past
when all is but a vague memento on the fringe of sky
you will revive little one
among the cinders
all along the line
of the new stations of our modest destiny
my poetry of the battered heart
my poetry of the rattling stones

— *Tr. by D. G. Jones*

Il est triste et pêle-mêle dans les étoiles tombées
livide, muet, nulle part et effaré, vaste fantôme
il est ce pays seul avec lui-même et neiges et rocs
un pays que jamais ne rejoint le soleil natal
en lui beau corps s'enfouit un sommeil désaltérant
pareil à l'eau dans la soif vacante des graviers

je le vois à la bride des hasards, des lendemains
il affleure dans les songes des hommes de peine
quand il respire en vagues de sous-bois et fougères
quand il brûle en longs peupliers d'années et d'oubli
l'inutile chlorophylle de son amour sans destin
quand gît à son coeur de misaine un désir d'être

il attend, prostré, il ne sait plus quelle rédemption
parmi les paysages qui marchent en son immobilité
parmi ses haillons de silence aux iris de mourant
il a toujours ce sourire échoué du pauvre avenir avili
il est toujours à sabrer avec les pagaies de l'ombre
l'horizon devant lui recule en avalanches de promesses

démuni, il ne connaît qu'un espoir de terrain vague
qu'un froid de jonc parlant avec le froid de ses os
le malaise de la rouille, l'à-vif, les nerfs, le nu
dans son large dos pâle les coups de couteaux cuits
il vous regarde, exploité, du fond de ses carrières
et par à travers les tunnels de son absence, un jour
n'en pouvant plus y perd à jamais la mémoire d'homme

(continued)

Sad and pitched about among the fallen stars
livid, mute, nowhere and afraid, vast ghost
it is this land alone with itself and winds and rocks
a land forever orphaned from its native sun
great body in which soothing sleep has gone to ground
like water in the empty thirst of gravel

I see it bridled by chance, by tomorrows
its dreams rising flush with the dreams of day laborers
while it breathes in waves of underbrush, dense bracken
burns through long years of poplar and neglect
the useless chlorophyll of its love without issue
shrouding in its mizzen heart the rage to be

prostrate it attends it knows not what redemption
amid wild tracts unfolding in its own inertia
amid rags of silence, irised like dying men
always it wears the failed smile of the future bankrupt
always it goes slashing about with paddles of darkness
the horizon receding always in an avalanche of promises

bereft it knows only the blank map of hope
the cold of reed-beds chatting with the cold of bone
distemper of rust, the quick, the nerve, nakedness
the heated blade, the blows in its broad pale back
it stares at you, exploited, from the depths of its quarries
through tunnels of absence, someday, spent
to lose forever the memory of man

(continued)

les vents qui changez les sorts de place la nuit
vents de rendez-vous, vents aux prunelles solaires
vents telluriques, vents de l'âme, vents universels
vents ameutez-nous, et de vos bras de fleuve ensemble
enserrez son visage de peuple abîmé, redonnez-lui
la chaleur
     et la profuse lumière des sillages d'hirondelles

winds that in the night are rearranging fates
nodal winds, winds with solar eyes
winds of the earth and of the spirit, universal winds
mass us winds and with your rivering arms meld
with one face this people, downcast, make it glow
with new warmth
      light spilling from the swallows' wake

— Tr. by D. G. Jones

Jamais je n'ai fermé les yeux
malgré les vertiges sucrés des euphories
même quand mes yeux sentaient le roussi
même en butte aux rafales montantes du sommeil

— Car je trempe jusqu'à la moelle des os
jusqu'aux états d'osmose incandescents
dans la plus noire transparence de nos sommeils

— Tapi au fond de moi tel le fin renard
alors je me résorbe en jeux, je mime et parade
ma vérité, le mal d'amour, et douleurs et joies

Et je m'écris sous la loi d'émeute
je veux saigner sur vous par toute l'affection
j'écris, j'écris, à faire un fou de moi
à me faire le fou du roi de chacun
volontaire aux enchères de la déraison
mon rire en volées de grelots par vos têtes
en chavirées de pluie dans vos jambes

Mais je ne peux me déprendre du conglomérat
je suis le rouge-gorge de la forge
le mégot de survie, l'homme agonique

Un jour de grande détresse à son comble
je franchirai les tonnerres des désespoirs
je déposerai ma tête exsangue sur un meuble
ma tête grenade et déflagration
sans plus de vue je continuerai, j'irai
vers ma mort peuplée de rumeurs et d'éboulis
je retrouverai ma nue propriété

THE AGONIZED MAN

Never have I shut my eyes
despite the sweet giddiness of euphoria
and even when I could feel them smoldering
even when I stood in sleep's rioting winds, never

— For down to my bone's marrow
down to those twilight osmotic states I am steeped
in the jetblack transparency of the stupor we live in

— Crouched inside myself then like a fox
I am absorbed in games, I mime and show
off my truth, love's heartache, and pains and joys

And I sign my name under the riot act
I want to bleed my affection on you
I write now I write to make a fool of myself
to be everyone's royal jester
ready at derision's bidding
my laughter like bells round your heads
like rain barreling through your legs

But I cannot part from the conglomerate
I am the red robin in the forge
the ground-out butt still burning, the agonized man

On my very worst possible day
I'll come through all of despair's thunder
lay my anemic head on a table at last
my head a bombshell and a blaze
seeing nothing I'll continue, I'll
go toward my death crowded with rumors and debris
I will have my bare property again

— *Tr. by Marc Plourde*

[31]

Homme aux labours des brûlés de l'exil
selon ton amour aux mains pleines de rudes conquêtes
selon ton regard arc-en-ciel arc-bouté dans les vents
en vue de villes et d'une terre qui te soient natales

je n'ai jamais voyagé
vers autre pays que toi mon pays

un jour j'aurai dit oui à ma naissance
j'aurai du froment dans mes yeux
je m'avancerai sur un sol, ému, ébloui
par la pureté de bête que soulève la neige

un homme reviendra
d'en dehors du monde

FOR MY REPATRIATION

Tiller of the scorched fields of exile, governed
by your love whose hands are full of crude conquests
by your rainbow-gaze arc-ended in the winds
anticipating cities and a land that could be yours

my country
I have never travelled
towards any country but you

the day will come when I can confess my birth
I will have wheatfields in my eyes
I will go forth on a soil, impassioned and dazzled
by the savage innocence upheaved by the snow

a man will return
from beyond the world

— *Tr. by Brenda Fleet*

Une idée ça vrille et pousse
l'idée du champ dans l'épi de blé
au coeur des feuilles l'idée de l'arbre
qui va faire une forêt
et même, même
forcenée, l'idée du chiendent

c'est dans l'homme tenu
sa tourmente aiguisée
sa brave folie grimpante
à hue, et à dia

Non, ça n'déracine pas
ça fait à sa tête de travers
cette idée-là, bizarre! qu'on a
tête de caboche, ô liberté

HARDHEADS

An idea spirals and burrows
the field idea in an ear of wheat
the tree idea that becomes a forest
camouflaged in its leaves
and even, even
growing wild, the crab-grass idea

and men held captive will have it
that fine-edged torment, that courageous
craziness sprouting up
and climbing everywhere at once

You can tell by their twisted noggins
and the damned thing
can't be weeded out, strange!
that idea we hardheads have got, O freedom

— Tr. by Marc Plourde

I

l fait un temps fou de soleil carrousel
la végétation de l'ombre partout palpitante
le jour qui promène les calèches du bonheur
le ciel qui est en marche sur des visages d'escale
puis le vent s'éprend au hasard d'un arbre seul
il allume tous les rêves de son feuillage

Belle vie où nos mains foisonnent je te coupe
je reçois en plein coeur tes objets qui brillent
voici des silences comme des révolvers éteints
mes yeux à midi comme des étangs tranquilles
les fleurs sont belles de la santé des femmes

Le temps mon amour le temps ramage de toi
continûment je te parle à voix de passerelles
beaucoup de gens murmurent ton nom de bouquet
je sais ainsi que tu es toujours la plus jolie
et naissante comme les beautés de chaque saison
il fait un monde heureux foulé de vols courbes

Je monte dans les échelles tirées de mes regards
je t'envoie mes couleurs vertes de forêt caravelle
il fait un temps de cheval gris qu'on ne voit plus
il fait un temps de château très tard dans la braise
il fait un temps de lune dans les sommeils lointains

I

The weather is crazy with a carousel sun
the vegetation of the shadow palpitating everywhere
the day brings out the carriages of happiness
the sky is promenading on the faces of the ports
then the wind falls in love by chance with a single tree
illuminating all the dreams in its foliage

Beautiful life where our hands grow in abundance I cut you down
I receive with a full heart your shining objects
here are silences like extinguished revolvers
my eyes at midday like tranquil pools
the flowers are beautiful like the strength of women

The weather my love the weather is a song about you
I speak to you continually with the rumbling of bridges
many people murmur your name that is like a bouquet
this is how I know that you are always the prettiest
and new-born like the beauties of each season
it is a happy world crowded with curved flights

I climb on the ladders extended from my gaze
I send you the green colors of the caravel forest
the weather is a grey horse that one no longer sees
it is a castle very late in the embers
it is like a moon in distant sleeps

II

Le vent rend l'âme dans un amas d'ombre
les étoiles bourdonnent dans leurs feux d'abeilles
et l'air est doux d'un passage d'écureuil
et même si le monde assiège nos solitudes
tu es belle et belle comme des ruses de renard

Lorsque fraîche et buvant les rosées d'envol
comme un ciel défaillant tu viens t'allonger
par le vieux silence animal de la plaine
mes paumes te portent comme la mer
en un tourbillon du coeur dans le corps entier

II

The wind gives up the ghost in a heap of shadows
the stars are humming in their bee-like flames
and the air is soft as a squirrel's passing
and even if the world lays siege to our solitudes
you are beautiful as beautiful as the cunning of a fox

When fresh and drinking the dews of flight
like a fading sky you come to stretch yourself
by the old animal silence of the plain
my palms carry you like the sea
in a whirlwind of the heart in the whole body

III

Toi qui m'aimes au hasard de toi-même
toi ma frégate nénuphar mon envolée libellule
le printemps s'épand en voiliers de paupières
voyageuse d'air léger de rêves céréales
bariolée avec tes robes aux couleurs
de perroquets bizarres
lieu d'arc-en-ciel et de blason
tempête de miel et de feu et moi
braque et balai
coeur tonnant et chevauché
par le brouhaha des sens
ta poitrine d'étincelles vertige voltige
et dans nos cambrures et nos renverses
mon corps t'enhoule
de violentes délices à tes hanches
et à grandes embardées de chevreuil de kayak
le monde bascule trinque et culbute
toi ma gigoteuse
toi ma giboyeuse

mon accotée
ma tanante de belle accotée

tes cils retiennent de vacillantes douceurs

III

You who love me at hazard to yourself
you my water-lily frigate my dragon-fly flight
spring extends in the sails of eyelids
voyager in the light air with its dreams of grain
gaudily painted with your dresses colored
like bizarre parrots
place of the rainbow and coat-of-arms
tempest of honey and fire and myself
mad joker and broom
heart that is thundering and ridden
by the hubbub of the senses
your breast made of sparks grows faint it leaps
and in our curves and our doublings
my body sends swells
of extreme pleasure to your haunches
and great lurches like the skin of a kayak
the world see-saws clinks somersaults
you my leg-shaker
you my hunting ground

my wall for leaning on
my beautiful hide for leaning on

your eyelashes contain sweet thoughts that come and go

— *Tr. by Louis Simpson*

Tu fus quelques nuits d'amour en mes bras
et beaucoup de vertige, beaucoup d'insurrection
même après tant d'années de mer entre nous
à chaque aube il est dur de ne plus t'aimer

parfois dans la foule, surgit l'éclair d'un visage
blanc comme fut naguère le tien dans ma tourmente
autour de moi l'air est plein de trous bourdonnant
peut-être qu'ailleurs passent sur ta chair désolée
pareillement des éboulis de bruits vides
et fleurissent les mêmes brûlures éblouissantes

si j'ai ma part d'incohérence il n'empêche
que par moment ton absence fait rage
qu'à travers cette absence je me désoleille
par mauvaise affliction et sale vue malade
j'ai un corps en mottes de braise où griffe
un mal fluide de glace vive en ma substance

ces temps difficiles malmènent nos consciences
le monde file un mauvais coton, et moi
tel le bec du pivert sur l'écorce des arbres
de déraison en désespoir mon coeur s'acharne
et comme lui, mitraillette, il martèle

ta lumière n'a pas fini de m'atteindre
ce jour-là, ma nouvellement oubliée
je reprendrai haut-bord et destin de poursuivre
en un femme aimée pour elle à cause de toi

[42]

You were a few nights of love in my arms
and dizziness, much rebellion
even after so many years with the sea between us
with each new dawn it is hard to stop loving you

sometimes in a crowd, a face strikes like lightning
white as yours seemed once in my anguish
and around me the air is full of hollow thunder
and elsewhere perhaps, on your grieving flesh
you too feel these rumbles of useless sound
and the same white flashes surround you

if I have my share of madness, it is no protection
from the moment when your absence rages
when through this absence I am clouded over
by a mean affliction and a sickened outlook
glowing embers mottle my body,
icy needles of poison claw through me

these difficult times play havoc with consciences
the world is in a bad way, and as for me
like a woodpecker's beak on tree-bark
my heart goes incessantly from madness to despair
and like this bird-machine-gun, hammers away

your light still goes on reaching me
but come the day when you are newly forgotten
I will openly pursue my destiny again
in a woman loved for herself because of you

— Tr. by Brenda Fleet

Si tant que dure l'amour
j'ai eu noir
j'ai eu froid
tellement souvent
tellement longtemps
si tant que femme s'en va
il fait encore
encore plus noir
encore plus froid
tellement toujours
toujours tellement

TWO SOLITUDES

As long as love lasts
I'm in the dark
I'm out in the cold
so many times
so long a time
and as often as a woman leaves me
I have it all to do again
even more in the dark
even more in the cold
it is always this way
it is always so

— Tr. by Brenda Fleet

Je vis dans une très vieille maison où je commence
à ressembler aux meubles, à la très vieille peau des fauteuils
peu à peu j'ai perdu toute trace de moi sur place
le temps me tourne et retourne dans ses bancs de brume
tête davantage pluvieuse, ma très-très tête au loin

    (Etais-je ces crépitements
    d'yeux en décomposition
    étais-je ce gong du coeur
    dans l'errance de l'avenir
    ou était-ce ma mort invisible pêchant à la ligne
    dans l'horizon visible . . .

    cependant qu'il m'arrive encore des fois
    de plus en plus brèves et distantes
    de surgir sur le seuil de mon visage
    entre chaleur et froid)

RUE SAINT-CHRISTOPHE

I live in a very old house where I am beginning
to resemble the furniture, the very old skin of armchairs
little by little I have lost all trace of myself in this place
time works upon me and brings back its fog-banks
my head rainier than ever my very distant head

    (Was I those cracklings
    of decomposing eyes
    was I that gong of the heart
    in the wandering of the future
    or was I my invisible death fishing with a line
    in the visible horizon . . .

    nevertheless it still happens at moments
    that are becoming more and more brief and distant
    to rise up on the threshold of my face
    between heat and cold)

— Tr. by Louis Simpson

J'ai la trentaine à brides abattues dans ma vie
je vous cherche encore pâturages de l'amour
je sens le froid humain de la quarantaine d'années
qui fait glace en dedans, et l'effroi m'agite . . .

je suis malheureux ma mère mais moins que toi
toi mes chairs natales, toi qui d'espérance t'insurges
ma mère au cou penché sur ton chagrin d'haleine
et qui perds gagnes les mailles du temps à tes mains

dans un autre temps mon père est devenu du sol
il s'avance en moi avec le goût du fil et des outils
mon père, ma mère, vous saviez à vous-deux nommer
toutes choses sur la terre, ô mon père, ô ma mère

  j'entends votre paix
  se poser comme la neige . . .

I'm thirty, the reins down in mid-career
and still looking to find love's pasture
I feel the human chill of the forties forming
an ice within, and fear shakes me . . .

I'm not happy but less, mother, unhappy
than you, my flesh, from hope always rebounding
you, mother, head bent above the sorrowful breath
hands dropping catching the stitches of time

in one of those stitches my father became earth
he moves now in me, my desire for sons, and tools
my father, my mother, together you could name
all things on earth, O father, O mother

    I hear your peace
    settling like the snow

— Tr. by D. G. Jones

Certains soirs d'hiver, lorsque, dehors, comme nouvellement
l'espace est emporté ici et là avec des ressacs de branches,
avec des rues, des abattis de poudrerie, puis, par moments,
avec de grands cratères de vide au bout du vent culbuté mort,
il fait nuit dans la neige même
les maisons voyagent chacune pour soi

et j'entends dans l'intimité de la durée
et tenant ferme les mancherons du pays
le vieil Ossian aveugle qui chante dans les radars

Certain winter nights, when, outside,
as of late
space is carried here and there with undertows
of branches,
with streets, barricades of snowswirls,
then at times,
with large craters of emptiness at the wind's end
capsized dead,
night falls in the snow itself
houses journey each on their own

and I hear in the intimacy of duration
firmly holding the country's plows
blind old Ossian who is singing in the radar

— *Tr. by Dennis Egan*

I

Me voici de nouveau dans le non-amour sans espace
avec mon amour qui dévale tel le chevreuil atteint
et comme la marée se retire pour la dernière fois
avec ma vie incertaine et dépaysée de terrain vague
avec mon corps en cendres et mes yeux en dedans
ô amour, fille, avec encore un peu de ta chaleur dorée
le vent m'emporte dans les souffles de nulle part

Et plus tard dans cette rue où je m'égare
éparpillé dans mes gestes et brouillé dans mon être
tombant et me soulevant dans l'âme
toute la pluie se rassemble sur mes épaules
la tristesse du monde luit très lasse et très basse
mais toi tristesse des hautes flammes dans mes genoux
tu me ravages comme les tourmentes des forêts rageuses
et parfois je me traîne et parfois je rafale . . .

II

Mais même dans l'en-dehors du temps de l'amour
dans l'après-mémoire des corps et du coeur
je ne suis revenu ni de tout ni de rien
je n'ai pas peur de pleurer en d'autres fois
je suis un homme irrigué, irriguant
de nouveau je m'avance vers toi, amour, je te demande
passage, amour je te demande demeure

I

Here I am again in the nowhere of love's absence
my love is leaving like a wounded deer, going
like the tide for the last time and here I am
in the strange wasteland of my life, body in ashes
eyes looking in and O my love, my girl, here I am
with still a little of your warmth's golden afterglow
as the wind carries me on its breath from nowhere

And later on this street where I lose myself
wasted from effort and the tangle of being
falling and rising in my soul
all the rain gathers on my shoulders
and the world's sadness glows very faint and faraway
but you my sadness are wildfire round my knees
you ravage me like a storm in a raging forest
and sometimes I stagger, oh stagger, or rush like the wind . . .

II

But even beyond love's time and even
in the after-memory of our bodies and feelings
I am not indifferent
I'm not afraid to cry again
I am a man who's been flooded and in a flood
I come toward you again, love, and I ask you
to let me pass, my love and ask you can I stay

— *Tr. by Marc Plourde*

Tu as les yeux pers des champs de rosées
tu as des yeux d'aventure et d'années-lumières
la douceur du fond des brises au mois de mai
pour les accompagnements de ma vie en friche
avec cette chaleur d'oiseau à ton corps craintif
moi qui suis charpente et beaucoup de fardoches
moi je fonce à vive allure et entêté d'avenir
la tête en bas comme un bison dans son destin
la blancheur des nénuphars s'élève jusqu'à ton cou
pour la conjuration de mes manitous maléfiques
moi qui ai des yeux où ciel et mer s'influencent
pour la réverbération de ta mort lointaine
avec cette tache errante de chevreuil que tu as

You have the blue-green eyes of fields in dew
adventurous eyes in which the light-years shine
you have the soft airs of winds in May
that birdlike from your timorous body play
an accompaniment through my uncleared fields
I who am timber and heaped brush
I who am drunk with the future, rush
headlong like a buffalo into his fate
the white of waterlilies rises to your throat
to conjure the dark manitous rising in my pulse
I in whose eyes the sea and sky conspire
for the reverberations of your far off death
in the telltale mark of the roe deer, your errant flesh

tu viendras toute ensoleillée d'existence
la bouche envahie par la fraîcheur des herbes
le corps mûri par les jardins oubliés
où tes seins sont devenus des envoûtements
tu te lèves, tu es l'aube dans mes bras
où tu changes comme les saisons
je te prendrai marcheur d'un pays d'haleine
à bout de misères et à bout de démesures
je veux te faire aimer la vie notre vie
t'aimer fou de racines à feuilles et grave
de jour en jour à travers nuits et gués
de moellons nos vertus silencieuses
je finirai bien par te rencontrer quelque part
contre tout ce qui me rend absent et douloureux
par le mince regard qui me reste au fond du froid
j'affirme ô mon amour que tu existes
je corrige notre vie

all sunlit with existence you will come
your mouth beseiged by all the freshness of the grass
your body ripened in forgotten gardens
flowering in the incantations of your breasts
you rise, you are the morning breaking in my arms
to grow and change there as the seasons change
brave walker in a land of breath
I will take you to the end of this distress
I will take you to the end of all excess
I want to make you fall in love with life, our life
to love you madly, root and branch, and gravely
day by day, across the nights and across
the stony fords of our mute righteousness
I will meet you in the end, somewhere, some place
in spite of everything that makes me absent, ache
with the meagre vision that is left me in the depths of cold
I affirm o my love that you exist
I correct our life

nous n'irons plus mourir de langueur mon amour
à des milles de distance dans nos rêves bourrasques
des filets de sang dans la soif craquelée de nos lèvres
les épaules baignées de vols de mouettes
non
j'irai te chercher nous vivrons sur la terre
la détresse n'est pas incurable qui fait de moi
une épave de dérision, un ballon d'indécence
un pitre aux larmes d'étincelles et de lésions profondes
frappe l'air et le feu de mes soifs
coule-moi dans tes mains de ciel de soie
la tête la première pour ne plus revenir
si ce n'est pour remonter debout à ton flanc
nouveau venu de l'amour de monde
constelle-moi de ton corps de voie lactée
même si j'ai fait de ma vie dans un plongeon
une sorte de marais, une espèce de rage noire
si je fus cabotin, concasseur de désespoir
j'ai quand même idée farouche
de t'aimer pour ta pureté
de t'aimer pour une tendresse que je n'ai pas connue

no more will we die of listlessness my love
before the endless miles in the squalls of our dreams
nor in the nets of blood, thirst's crackling on our lips
our shoulders bathed in flights of gulls
no
I will set out to find you, we will live on the earth
these straits that have reduced me to a drifting hulk
a balloon to be obscenely pricked, a clown
with starry tears and deeper wounds, are not invincible
beat up the air, beat up the fire of my desires
run me through the silken skies of your hands
headfirst, preventing my return
except I mount again becoming upright at your side
the newcomer sprung from the love of the world
constellate me in your body's milky way
even if I've made of my life's plunge
a sort of swamp, a kind of black rage
have been a wandering ham, gravel-crusher of despair
even so I am ferociously inclined
to love you still, to love you for your purity
and for a tenderness that I have never known

dans les giboulées d'étoiles de mon ciel
l'éclair s'épanouit dans ma chair
je passe les poings durs au vent
j'ai un coeur de mille chevaux-vapeur
j'ai un coeur comme la flamme d'une chandelle
toi tu as la tête d'abîme douce n'est-ce pas
la nuit de saule dans tes cheveux
un visage enneigé de hasards et de fruits
un regard entretenu de sources cachées
et mille chants d'insectes dans tes veines
et mille pluies de pétales dans tes caresses

In sudden showers, stars bursting from my sky
the lightning streams through my flesh
and I go on fists clenched in the wind
a thousand horsepower beating in my heart
and in my heart a candle's flame
and you, your head holds all the mystery of a sweet abyss
is that not so
your hair the night of willow trees
your face is dusted with the snows
and fruits of fortune, and your gaze
is held still mistress to the hidden springs
and in your veins a thousand insects sing
and in your manifold caress a thousand petals rain

tu es mon amour
ma clameur mon bramement
tu es mon amour ma ceinture fléchée d'univers
ma danse carrée des quatre coins d'horizon
le rouet des écheveaux de mon espoir
tu es ma réconciliation batailleuse
mon murmure de jours à mes cils d'abeille
mon eau bleue de fenêtre
dans les hauts vols de buildings
mon amour
de fontaines de haies de ronds-points de fleurs
tu es ma chance ouverte et mon encerclement
à cause de toi
mon courage est un sapin toujours vert
et j'ai du chiendent d'achigan plein l'âme
tu es belle de tout l'avenir épargné
d'une frêle beauté soleilleuse contre l'ombre
ouvre-moi tes bras que j'entre au port
et mon corps d'amoureux viendra rouler
sur les talus du Mont-Royal
orignal, quand tu brames orignal
coule-moi dans ta palinte osseuse
fais-moi passer tout cabré tout empanaché
dans ton appel et ta détermination
Montréal est grand comme un désordre universel
tu es assise quelque part avec l'ombre et ton coeur
ton regard vient luire sur le sommeil des colombes
fille dont le visage est ma route aux réverbères
quand je plonge dans les nuits de sources
si jamais je te rencontre fille
après les femmes de la soif glacée

(continued)

you are my love
my clamouring hooves, my bellowing
you are my love, my winter sash, orbiting the air
you are my square dance at the four corners of the world
my hank of hope, my spinning wheel
you are my deal
my fighting resolution to be reconciled
you are the hum of days before my grilled bee's eyes
my window of blue water in the high
flights of buildings, cries, my love
of fountains, hedges, traffic circles filled with flowers
you are my chance in life, my prison yard
because of you
my courage is a spruce, forever green
my spirit's backboned with the rock bass
for you are beautiful
with all the spendings of the days to come
investing with frail sunlight all the poverty of dark
open your arms that I may enter port
my lover's body roll upon the talus of Mount Royal
my bellowing an echo to your bell
inhale me through your bony throat
and make me rear, parade in the panache
of your appeal and your determination
Montreal is large as all the world's disorder
somewhere in its shadows you are sitting and your heart
your gaze lights up the sleep of doves
girl whose face is now my lamplit route
as in the depths I plunge into the midnight springs
if ever I encounter you, my girl
after all these women with their icy thirst

(continued)

je pleurerai te consolerai
de tes jours sans pluies et sans quenouilles
des hasards de l'amour dénoué
j'allumerai chez toi les phares de la douceur
nous nous reposerons dans la lumière
de toutes les mers en fleurs de manne
puis je jetterai dans ton corps le vent de mon sang
tu seras heureuse fille heureuse
d'être la femme que tu es dans mes bras
le monde entier sera changé en toi et moi

I will console you with my tears
for the days without rain or rushes green or thread to spin
for the risks of love once it's unwound
and I will light for you great lamps of tenderness
and we shall rest
in the light of seas flowering in manna
then will I unleash
within your body all the winds of my blood
you will rejoice, my girl, you will rejoice
to be the woman that you are in my arms
the world in us will be transformed

la marche à l'amour s'ébruite en un voilier
de pas voletant par les eaux blessées de nénuphars
mes absolus poings
ah violence de délices et d'aval
j'aime
      que j'aime
            que tu t'avances
ma ravie
frileuse aux pieds nus sur les frimas
par ce temps doucement entêté de perce-neige
sur ces grèves où l'été
pleuvent en longues flammèches les cris des pluviers
harmonica du monde lorsque tu passes et cèdes
ton corps tiède de pruche à mes bras pagayeurs
lorsque nous gisons fleurant la lumière incendiée
et qu'en tangage de moisson ourlée de brises
je me déploie sur ta fraîche chaleur de cigale
je roule en toi
tous les saguenays d'eau noire de ma vie
je fais naître en toi
les frénésies de frayères au fond du coeur d'outaouais
puis le cri de l'engoulevent vient s'abattre dans ta gorge
terre meuble de l'amour ton corps
se soulève en tiges pêle-mêle
je suis au centre du monde tel qu'il gronde en moi
avec la rumeur de mon âme dans tous les coins
je vais jusqu'au bout des comètes de mon sang
haletant
      harcelé de néant
            et dynamité
de petites apocalypses
les deux mains dans les furies dans les féeries
ô mains
ô poings
comme des cogneurs de folles tendresses

[66]

the advance toward love now spreads to sail
with quivering stride on the waters wounded with lilies
my absolute fists
oh the violence of downstream, whirling delight
I love
        how I love
                how you advance
my ecstasy
shivering barefoot in the glittering frosts
in this season sweetly studded with snowdrops
on these shores where summer rains down
in long flakes the fiery cries of the plover
harmonica of the world as you pass and yield
your body warm as the birch bark in my paddler's arms
as we lie still, scenting the air in the burning light
as in the pitching harvest woven by the gales
I unfold in your warmth to the long cry of the cicada
in you I roll
my Saguenays, all the black waters of my life
in you I beget
the frenzies of the spawning grounds in the heart of the Ottawa
the cry of the nighthawk comes to beat in your throat
the earth, love's furniture, your flesh
erupt pell mell in fresh shoots
I am the center of the world as it groans
from the four corners of the globe with the rumor of my soul
I go to the very end of all the comets of my blood
panting
        harassed by the void
                dynamited
by a chronic small apocalypse
both hands in the fury of the storm, in fairyland
o hands
of fists
like hammers in a mad caress

[67]

mais que tu m'aimes et si tu m'aimes
s'exhalera le froid natal de mes poumons
le sang tournera ô grand cirque
je sais que tout amour
sera retourné comme un jardin détruit
qu'importe je serai toujours si je suis seul
cet homme de lisière à bramer ton nom
éperdûment malheureux parmi les pluies de trèfles
mon amour ô ma plainte
de merle-chat dans la nuit buissonneuse
ô fou feu froid de la neige
beau sexe floral ô ma neige
mon amour d'éclairs lapidée
morte
dans le froid des plus lointaines flammes

because you love me and if you love me
the frost that was born in my lungs will breathe away
my blood will revolve o magnificent circus
I know that love
will always be returned like a garden destroyed
what does it matter if I am alone I will always
be this marginal man belling your name
madly unhappy amid showers of sweet clover
my love o my complaint
of the catbird crying in the bushy night
sweet fool sweet fire sweet cold of the snow
o floral sex, my snow
my love defamed by the lightning stoned
dead
in the cold of the most distant flames

puis les années m'emportent sens dessus dessous
je m'en vais en délabre au bout de mon rouleau
des voix murmurent les récits de ton domaine
à part moi je me parle
que vais-je devenir dans ma force fracassée
ma force noire du bout de mes montagnes
pour te voir à jamais je déporte mon regard
je me tiens aux écoutes des sirènes
dans la longue nuit effilée du clocher de Saint-Jacques
et parmi ces bouts de temps qui halètent
me voici de nouveau campé dans ta légende
tes grands yeux qui voient beaucoup de cortèges
les chevaux de bois de tes rires
tes yeux de paille et d'or
seront toujours au fond de mon coeur
et ils traverseront les siècles

so willy nilly I am driven by the years
and I go on, run ragged, to the end of my rope
voices around me rumour your estate
and I say to myself
what's to become of me in my broken strength
my dark strength draining from my mountain base
to see you always I avert my sight
I stand alert for sirens in the long night
unwinding from the bell tower of St. James
and in these whereabouts of time that pant
here I am again, my camp pitched amid your legend
your wide eyes that look out on so many processions
the painted horses of your laughter
your straw-flecked eyes, your gold eyes —
they will always be there in the bottom of my heart
they will travel through centuries by that art

je marche à toi
je titube à toi
je meurs de toi jusqu'à la complète anémie
lentement je m'affale tout au long de ma hampe
je marche à toi, je titube à toi, je bois
à la gourde vide du sens de la vie
à ces pas semés dans les rues sans nord ni sud
à ces taloches de vent sans queue et sans tête
je n'ai plus de visage pour l'amour
je n'ai plus de visage pour rien de rien
parfois je m'assois par pitié de moi
j'ouvre mes bras à la croix des sommeils
mon corps est un dernier réseau de tics amoureux
avec à mes doigts les ficelles des souvenirs perdus
je n'attends pas à demain je t'attends
je n'attends pas la fin du monde je t'attends
dégagé de la fausse auréole de ma vie

I stride to you
reel to you
die for you even to the point of complete inanition
slowly I sink the whole length of my shaft
I stride to you, reel to you, drink
from the gourd emptied of meaning
with these steps sown in the street without north or south
with these cuffs of the wind without heads or tails
I have no more face for love
I have no more face for anything at all
sometimes I sit down out of kindness to myself
I open my arms to the cross of sleep
my body the last network of amorous tics
at my fingers threads of fond memories lost
I no longer wait for tomorrow, I wait for you
I no longer wait for the end of the world, I wait for you
detached from the false halo of my life

— Tr. by D. G. Jones

Corneille, ma noire
corneille qui me saoule
opaque et envoûtante
venue pour posséder ta saison et ta descendance

Déjà l'été goûte un soleil de mûres
déjà tu conjoins en ton vol la terre et l'espace
au plus bas de l'air de même qu'en sa hauteur
et dans le profond des champs et des clôtures
s'éveille dans ton appel l'intimité prochaine
du grand corps brûlant de juillet

Corneille, ma noire
parmi l'avril friselis

Avec l'alcool des chaleurs nouvelles
la peau s'écarquille et tu me rends
bric-à-brac sur mon aire sauvage et fou braque
dans tous les coins et recoins de moi-même
j'ai mille animaux et plantes par la tête
et cependant que tes larges battements
m'agitent en frondaisons de désirs
mon sang dans l'air remue comme une haleine

Corneille, ma noire
jusqu'en ma moelle

Tu me fais prendre la femme que j'aime
du même trébuchant et même
tragique croassement rauque et souverain
dans l'immémoriale et la réciproque
secousse des corps
Corneille, ma noire

THE RAVEN

Raven, my black beauty
raven like a shot of liquor
shadowy and spellbinding here
you've come to claim your season and your lineage

Already summer tastes of a mulberry sun
already you marry heaven and earth in your flight
near to the ground and high in the air
and far away in the fields and on the fences
the coming intimacy of July's great fiery body
is awakened by your call

Raven, my black beauty
amid April's rustling

Under the alcohol of this new heat
the skin stretches wide and you turn me
into a tangle wild and scatterbrained
in every nook and cranny of myself
a thousand animals and plants stir in my mind
and while your sleeping wings arouse
inside me the buds of desire
my blood in the air moves like a breath

Raven, my black beauty
to the very marrow

You make me take the woman I love
with the same quavering and with the same
tragic, raucous and sovereign cawing
in the jolt of bodies
in that immemorial and mutual tremor
Raven, my black beauty

— *Tr. by Marc Plourde*

Dans les lointains de ma rencontre des hommes
le coeur serré comme les maisons d'Europe
avec les maigres mots frileux de mes héritages
avec la pauvreté natale de ma pensée rocheuse

j'avance en poésie comme un cheval de trait
tel celui-là de jadis dans les labours de fond
qui avait l'oreille dressée à se saisir réel
les frais matins d'été dans les mondes brumeux

IN THE FAR OUT

In the far out of my encounters with men
the heart twice-barred like the houses of Europe
with my meagre inheritance of chill words
and the bare rocky thought to which I was born

I make it in poetry much like the workhorse
that once hauled stumps, broke land
that pricked up its ears to make sure it was real
those cool summer mornings in the misty worlds

— Tr. by D. G. Jones

L'homme de ce temps porte le visage de la flagellation
et toi, Terre de Québec, Mère Courage
dans ta longue marche, tu es grosse
de nos rêves charbonneux douloureux
de l'innombrable épuisement des corps et des âmes

je suis né ton fils en-haut là-bas
dans les vieilles montagnes râpées du nord
j'ai mal et peine ô morsure de naissance
cependant qu'en mes bras ma jeunesse rougeoie

voici mes genoux que les hommes nous pardonnent
nous avons laissé humilier l'intelligence des pères
nous avons laissé la lumière du verbe s'avilir
jusqu'à la honte et au mépris de soi dans nos frères
nous n'avons pas su lier nos racines de souffrance
à la douleur universelle dans chaque homme ravalé

je vais rejoindre les brûlants compagnons
dont la lutte partage et rompt le pain du sort commun
dans les sables mouvants des détresses grégaires

nous te ferons, Terre de Québec
lit de résurrections
et des milles fulgurances de nos métamorphoses
de nos levains où lève le futur
de nos volontés sans concessions
les hommes entendront battre ton pouls dans l'histoire
c'est nous ondulant dans l'automne d'octobre
c'est le bruit roux de chevreuils dans la lumière
l'avenir dégagé
        l'avenir engagé

OCTOBER

The man of the hour has the face of a scourged Christ
and you, Land of Quebec, Mother Courage
in your long march you are swollen
with our painful infectious dreams
with the uncounted wasting of bodies and souls

upland back there I was born
your son in the old grated mountains of the north
I hurt and ache with the bite of birth
while in my arms my youth blushes

here are my knees so that men may forgive us
we have allowed our fathers' spirit to be degraded
we have allowed the word's splendor to be debased
till we were ashamed and hating ourselves in our brothers
we didn't know how to bind our suffering's roots
to the universal pain in each man hollowed out

I will join my burning companions whose struggle
breaks and shares the bread of our common lot
in the quicksand huddles of grief

we will make you, Land of Quebec
a bed of resurrections
and a thousand lightning metamorphoses
of our leavens from which the future shall rise
and of our wills which will concede nothing
men shall hear your pulse beating through history
this is us winding through the October autumn
the russet sound of roe-deer in the sunlight
this is our future, clear
                    and committed

                                        — *Tr. by Marc Plourde*

Compagnon des Amériques
mon Québec ma terre amère ma terre amande
ma patrie d'haleine dans la touffe des vents
j'ai de toi la difficile et poignante présence
avec une large blessure d'espace au front
au-delà d'une vivante agonie de roseaux au visage

je parle avec les mots noueux de nos endurances
nous avons soif de toutes les eaux du monde
nous avons faim de toutes les terres du monde
dans la liberté criée de débris d'embâcle
nos feux de position s'allument vers le large
l'aïeule prière de nos doigts défaillante
la pauvreté luisant comme des fers à nos chevilles

mais cargue-moi en toi pays, cargue-moi
et marche au rompt le coeur de tes écorces tendres
marche à l'arête de tes dures plaies d'érosion
marche à tes pas réveillés des sommeils d'ornières
et marche à ta force épissure des bras à ton sol

mais chante plus haut l'amour en moi, chante
je me ferai passion de ta face
je me ferai porteur des germes de ton espérance
veilleur, guetteur, coureur, haleur de ton avènement
un homme de ton réquisitoire
un homme de ta patience raboteuse et varlopeuse
un homme de ta commisération infinie

(continued)

Companion of the Americas
Quebec, my bitter land, my almond land
my breathing space in the tuft of winds
from you I take my difficult, my poignant stance
the wide wound of space on my brow
the living agony of reeds on my face

I speak with the knotted winds of our endurance
we have a thirst for all the waters of the world
we have a hunger for all the lands of the earth
with the liberty bell sounding amid the debris
        of the spring break-up
all our beacons light us toward the open sea
ancestral prayer flickering from our fingers
poverty glinting like irons on our ankles

but reef me in, my land, reef me in
and run close-hauled to shiver your timbers
run on the crest of your hard scars of erosion
run like the waters newly wakened from ruts
run with the electric junction of your arms
        in the earth

but sing up the love within me, sing
I will make of your face a passion
I will make of myself a carrier of the germ of
        your hope
vigilante, sentry, runner, a hauler and
        hailer of your coming
your man for the prosecution
your man for the patient planing and honing
your man for the endless commiserations

(continued)

[81]

l'homme artériel de tes gigues
dans le poitrail effervescent des poudreries
dans la grande artillerie de tes couleurs d'automne
dans tes hanches de montagnes
dans l'accord comète de tes plaines
dans l'artésienne vigueur de tes villes

devant toutes les litanies
    de chats-huants qui huent dans la lune
devant toutes les compromissions en peaux de vison
devant les héros de la bonne conscience
les émancipés malingres
    les insectes des belles manières
devant tous les commandeurs de ton exploitation
de ta chair à pavé
    de ta sueur à gages

mais donne la main à toutes les rencontres, pays
ô toi qui apparais
    par tous les chemins défoncés de ton histoire
aux hommes debout dans l'horizon de la justice
qui te saluent
salut à toi territoire de ma poésie
salut les hommes des pères de l'aventure

roadman of your every dance and jig
in the deep-chested effervescence of your snow squalls
in the heavy artillery of your autumn colours
in the thighs of your mountains
in the comely comets of your plains
in the artesian vigor of your towns

before all the litanies of alley-cats
        screeching in the moonlight
before all the compromises clothed in mink
before all the heroes of tender conscience
the emancipated malingerers
        the insects of good manners
before all the entrepreneurs of your exploitation
of your paved flesh
        of your wagered sweat

but give a hand to all encounters, country
land, O you who have emerged
        from all the pot-holed roads of your history
to all upright men on the horizon of justice
who salute you
hail to you *territoire de ma poésie*
hail, men born of the fathers of adventure

                                              — *Tr. by* D. G. *Jones*

Ma belle folie crinière au vent
je m'abandonne à toi sur les chemins
avec les yeux magiques du hibou
parmi les fous fins fils du mal monde
parce que moi le noir
                    moi le forcené
        magnifique

NATURAL HOME

My pretty folly mane in the wind
I give myself to you wholly taking the road
with the magic eyes of the owl
among all the fine fools bad bets bad seed
because dark horse myself
                              myself crazy horse

    oh magnificent

                                        — Tr. by D. G. Jones

Pour parler de toi à mes côtés
je retrouve ma voix pêle-mêle
la lévitation de ma force
et les jeux qui ne sont pas faits.

Par ces temps nous traversons ensemble
avec fracas et beauté de nos âges
la déréliction intime et publique

Et je te porte sur toute la surface de mon corps
comme Lascaux
moi pan de mur céleste

FOURTH LOVE

You at my side, to speak of it
pell mell I recover my voice
my strength, a levitation
and all the moves that have yet to be made

In this time, amid all the private
and public disarray, the racket and beauty
of our ages, together we make it

And I bear you on every part of my body
like a cave at Lascaux
my celestial rock-face

— Tr. by D. G. Jones

La mort trébuchera dans sa dernière moisson
nous ne sommes plus qu'un dernier brin d'herbe
en tête-à-tête avec la vie
puis le monde n'est plus qu'un souvenir de bulle

La mort trébuchera dans sa dernière moisson
la mort aux yeux de chavirements de ciel et terre
en petits coups des à-coups de vitesse aux manettes au
      volant des roues
en petites gorgées de secousses de laveuse de chemins
      carossables
en petits élans de kayak en descente et culbutes et
      cascades et toboggan
la mort la mort acétylène en fanaux de nuit
un matin d'obus lilas
en fraîcheur d'éclair et de truite mouchetée
la mort au cri de girouette dans la gorge
la mort elle ne pèse que l'ombre de l'ombre
femme ô femme petites âmes petites vagues petites suites
      de petits fracassements dans mes bras
de froissements de papier à cigarette
de frondaisons dans les frayères des voluptés
de feux doux s'épandant à l'infini du fini

et dans l'ombre de l'ombre de chaque nuit
dormir et s'aimer encore
ô dormir
fleurir ensemble

Death will stumble in its final harvest
now we thrill and bend with life like a last
remaining blade of grass
soon our world will be a bubble suspended in memory

Death will stumble in its final harvest
death that comes with eyes toppling heaven and earth
with little quick jolts shaking gearshift ignition
    and steering wheels
with little water jets washing the streets clean
with little kayak leaps bounds spins and toboggan
    somersaults
death acetylene death's headlights exploding
one morning in lilac shells
sparkling and flashing like a speckled trout
death's weather vane rattling in the throat
death that weighs no more than a shadow's shadow
woman O woman little souls little waves little
    chains of little shatterings in my arms
of rustling cigarette paper
of foliage in the spawnings of lush pleasures
of sweet fires stretching to the limit's limit

and in the shadow's shadow of each night
to sleep and love still
O sleep
and flower together

                        — Tr. by Marc Plourde

Ma pauvre poésie en images de pauvres
avec tes efforts les yeux sortis de l'histoire
avec tes efforts de collier au cou des délires
ma pauvre poésie dans tes nippes de famille
de quel front tu harangues tes frères humiliés
de quel droit tu vociferes ton sort avec eux
et ces charges de dynamite dans le cerveau
et ces charges de bison vers la lumière
lumière dans la gangue d'ignorance
lumière emmaillotée de crépuscule
n'est-ce pas de l'inusable espoir des pauvres
ma pauvre poésie tel un amour chez les humbles
de perce-neige malgré les malheurs de chacun
de perce-confusion de perce-aberration
ma pauvre poésie dont les armes rouillent
dans le haut côté de la mémoire
dans le gargouillement de ta parole
ma pauvre poésie toujours si près de t'évanouir
désespérée mais non pas résignée
obstinée dans ta compassion et le salut collectif
malgré les malheurs avec tous et entre nous
qu'ainsi à l'exemple des pauvres tu as ton orgueil
et comme des pauvres ensemble un jour tu seras
dans une conscience ensemble
sans honte et retrouvant une nouvelle dignité

LA PAUVRETÉ ANTHROPOS

My poor poetry with your images of the poor
with your efforts eyes that emerge from history
with your efforts heroic labor at the neck of delirium
my poor poetry in your family clothes
with what a countenance you harangue your humiliated brothers
with what right do you shout about the fate you share with them
and those charges of dynamite in the brain
and those bison charges at the light
light in the matrix of ignorance
light swaddled in twilight
does it not come of the enduring hope of the poor
my poor poetry such a love among the humble
flowers that pierce through the snow in spite of the
        misfortunes of each
of piercing through confusion and aberration
my poor poetry whose arms are rusting
in the high side of memory
in the rumbling of your word
my poor poetry always so ready to vanish
desperate but not resigned
obstinate in your compassion and collective security
in spite of the misfortunes with all and among ourselves
so that following the example of the poor you have your pride
and like the poor who stick together one day you will be
in the consciousness of the whole people
without shame and again finding a new dignity

— *Tr. by Louis Simpson*

Je demande pardon aux poètes que j'ai pillés
— poètes de tous pays, de toutes époques —
je n'avais pas d'autres mots, d'autres écritures
que les vôtres, mais d'une façon, frères
c'est un bien grand hommage à vous
car aujourd'hui, ici, d'un homme à l'autre
il y a des mots entre eux, qui sont
leur propre fil conducteur de l'homme
merci.

I ask forgiveness of those poets I've pilfered
— poets from every country and every age —
I didn't have any other words, any other writings
than yours, but, still my brothers
in a way it's a fine tribute to you
for today, here, from one man to another
now there are words between them
words that are man's own conductive wire
thank you.

— Tr. by Marc Plourde

Gaston Miron was born in Sainte-Agathe-des-Monts, Quebec, in 1928, and moved to Montreal in 1947, working at a variety of different jobs and taking evening courses in the social sciences. He soon became one of the central animators of a new Quebec literature. In 1953, with five other friends, he founded the publishing house, l'Hexagone, which became almost synonymous with the new Quebec poetry. In 1957, he was one of the principal organizers of what has since become a yearly gathering of Quebec writers. In 1959–60, he spent some time in Paris establishing contacts with French writers and exploring the publishing business. Throughout the next decades he was active in a variety of organizations promoting the French language, culture, and independent identity of Quebec. Following the joint publication, with Olivier Marchand, of *Deux Sangs* (1953), Miron presented his poetry in oral readings or in the pages of small reviews, until, in 1970, the editors of the magazine *Etudes françaises* awarded him a prize and also gathered many of his major texts, in poetry and prose, in the book *L'homme rapaillé*, certainly one of the central texts in modern Quebec literature, and recently republished by Maspero in France. *Courtepointes* (1975) gathers together a number of other, previously uncollected poems. Among a variety of awards, Miron won the Prix Guillaume Apollinaire in France in 1981 and the Molson Prize in Canada in 1985.

D. G. Jones was born in Bancroft, Ontario in 1929, and was educated at McGill and Queen's Universities. He has taught English in several Canadian universities and, since 1963, has been a member of the Départment des études anglaises at l'Université de Sherbrooke. He has published a critical study of Canadian literature, *Butterfly on Rock*, plus five books of poetry, including *Under the Thunder the Flowers Light up the Earth* (1977), which won the Michigan State University A. J. M. Smith prize for poetry as well as the Governor General's Award. A founding editor and frequent contributor to the magazine *Ellipse*, which is devoted to the translation of English and French-Canadian poetry, he translated a selection of the poetry of Paul-Marie Lapointe published by the International Poetry Forum under the title *The Terror of the Snows* (1976). (A slightly enlarged Canadian edition has just been published as *The Fifth Season*.) D. G. Jones lives in North Hatley, Quebec, not far from the Vermont border.